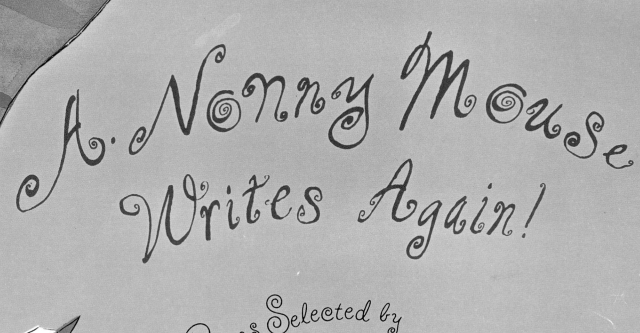

A. Nonny Mouse Writes Again!

Poems Selected by
Jack Prelutsky

Illustrated by
Marjorie Priceman

Dragonfly Books™

Alfred A. Knopf · New York

DRAGONFLY BOOKS™ PUBLISHED BY ALFRED A. KNOPF, INC.

Library of Congress Cataloging-in-Publication Data

Prelutsky, Jack.

A. Nonny Mouse writes again! / selected by Jack Prelutsky ; illustrated by Marjorie Priceman.

p.   cm.

Summary: Another illustrated collection of primarily traditional or anonymous verses, in such categories as "Wordplay," "Food," "Impossible Doings," and "Bad Kids."

ISBN 0-679-83715-9 (trade) — ISBN 0-679-93715-3 (lib. bdg.) — ISBN 0-679-88087-9 (pbk.)

1. Children's poetry, American. 2. Children's poetry, English. 3. Anonymous writings. [1. American poetry—Collections. 2. English poetry—Collections. 3. Anonymous writings.] I. Prelutsky, Jack. II. Priceman, Marjorie, ill.

PS586.3.A2 1993 811.008'09282—dc20 92-5214

http://www.randomhouse.com/

First Dragonfly Books Edition: December 1996

Printed in the United States of America

10 9 8 7 6 5 4 3 2

For Anna, Nick, and Peter — J. P.
For Diane, Jim, James, and Patrick — M. P.

Dear Mr. Prelutsky,

I was finishing my afternoon tea and musing over a last bit of toast when I decided it was high time to catch up with my correspondence. Ever since the publication of Poems of A. Nonny Mouse, I've received fan mail from admiring readers. Though I thoroughly enjoy perusing the letters, I must admit that it had become a bit of a chore keeping up with it all, especially since I do attempt to answer everyone. It sometimes makes me wish that I had learned to type—I wonder if it's too late?

I'd been scribbling replies for several hours when I realized that it's been months since you and I had heard from each other, and thought it might be nice to drop you this line and renew our friendship.

My life has improved quite a bit since our book went to press. Not only do I see more of my poems in print now, but more and more often they are being correctly attributed to me—instead of to "Anonymous." Furthermore, I've been able to afford the occasional wedge of imported cheese, have finally had the leaks in my roof repaired, and have even managed to put aside a little something for my old age. In fact, I've been so delighted with the results of our first collaboration that I thought we might get together again to compile another volume of my verse.

I've taken the liberty of sending you the enclosed poems, long forgotten, which I recently found in a misplaced notebook. In all modesty, I believe they are quite as good as those I originally sent you, and feel they justify a second collection.

By the way, I recently came across one of **your** poems, in the New York Times, mistakenly attributed to **me**. I was so embarrassed! I hope you won't hold this against me, as you have my word that I had nothing to do with the unfortunate error. Will publishers ever learn?

I trust you are in good health, and hope to hear from you soon.

Cordially,

A. Nonny Mouse

Ms. A. Nonny Mouse
Cheddarville, 1993

P.S. Many people commented on how much they enjoyed searching through our first book for the quartet of poems you wrote in a style approximating my own. If you decide to join me in producing a second volume, I do hope you will contribute another four verses.

Ten tom-toms,
Timpani, too,
Ten tall tubas
And an old kazoo.

Ten trombones—
Give them a hand!
The sitting-standing-marching-running
Big Brass Band.

As I was sitting in my chair
I knew the bottom wasn't there,
Nor legs nor back,
But I just sat,
Ignoring little things like that.

One fine October morning
In September, last July,
The moon lay thick upon the ground,
The snow shone in the sky.
The flowers were singing gaily,
The birds were in full bloom,
I went down to the cellar
To
sweep
the
upstairs
room.

There was a young woman named Bright,
Whose speed was much faster than light.
She set out one day
In a relative way
And returned on the previous night.

Awake, arise, pull out your eyes,
And hear what time of day.
And when you've done, pull out your tongue,
And see what you can say.

Methuselah ate what he found on his plate,
And never, as people do now,
Did he note the amount of the calorie count:
He ate it because it was chow.
He wasn't disturbed as at dinner he sat,
Devouring a roast or a pie,
To think it was lacking in granular fat
Or a couple of vitamins shy.
He cheerfully chewed each species of food,
Unmindful of troubles or fears
Lest his health might be hurt
By some fancy dessert—
And he lived over nine hundred years.

I scream,   you scream,   We all scream for ice cream.

Mr. East gave a feast,
Mr. North laid the cloth,
Mr. West did his best,
Mr. South burned his mouth
With eating a cold potato.

I had a little pup, his name was Spot,
Whenever we cooked, he licked the pot,
Whenever we ate, he never forgot
To lick the dishes as well as the pot.

Hannah Bantry
In the pantry,
Gnawing at a mutton bone.
How she gnawed it,
How she clawed it,
When she found herself alone.

Little Katy wandered where
She espied a grizzly bear.
Noticing his savage wrath,
Katy kicked him from her path.

Little Katy, darling child,
Met a leopard, fierce and wild.
Ere the ugly creature sped off,
Little Katy bit his head off.

Little Willie,
Pair of skates,
Hole in the ice,
Pearly gates.

My sister likes to gross me out,
And she knows how to do it —
She fills her mouth with sauerkraut
And makes me watch her chew it.

When Grandma visits you, my dears,
Be good as you can be.
Don't put hot waffles in her ears
Or beetles in her tea.

Don't sew a pattern on her cheek
With worsted or with silk.
Don't call her naughty names in Greek
Or spray her face with milk.

Don't drive a staple in her foot,
Don't stick pins in her head.
And, oh, I beg you, do not put
Live embers in her bed.

These things are not considered kind,
They worry her and tease.
Such cruelty is not refined —
It always fails to please.

Be good to Grandma, little chaps,
Whatever else you do.
And then she'll grow to be — perhaps —
More tolerant of you.

Our kitten, the one we call Louie,
Will never eat liver so chewy,
  Nor the milk, nor the fish
  That we put in his dish.
He only will dine on chop suey.

A mouse is of a tiny size,
An elephant's immense,
And though an owl is very wise,
A skunk has all the scents.

Consider the poor hippopotamus:
His life is unduly monotonous.
  He lives half asleep
  At the edge of the deep,
And his face is as big as his bottom is.

There was a hungry hunter
Went hunting for a hare,
But where he hoped the hare would be
He found a hairy bear!

He saw its eyes, he saw its claws,
He saw its teeth and then—
The hunter turned head over heels
And hurried home again.

Be kind to the moose.
He may be of use
For hanging your hat
Or something like that...

When Noah sailed the waters blue,
He had his troubles, same as you.
For forty days he drove his ark
Before he found a place to park.

Tiny surfer,
Bold and brave,
Surfed upon
A microwave.

Swan swam over the sea —
Swim, swan, swim.
Swan swam back again —
Well swam, swan.

I saw you in the ocean,
I saw you in the sea,
I saw you in the bathtub,
Oops! Pardon me.

Three wise men of Gotham,
They went to sea in a bowl.
And if the bowl had been stronger,
My song would be longer.

O Moon! When I look on your beautiful face
Careening along through the darkness of space,
The thought has quite frequently come to my mind
If ever I'll gaze on your lovely behind.

"Your teeth are like the stars," he said,
And pressed her hand so white.
He spoke the truth, for like the stars,
Her teeth came out at night.

When all the cows were sleeping,
And the sun had gone to bed,
Up jumped the scarecrow,
And this is what he said:

"I'm a dingle-dangle scarecrow
With a flippy-floppy hat.
I can shake my hands like this,
And I can shake my feet like that."

When all the hens were roosting,
And the moon behind a cloud,
Up jumped the scarecrow
And shouted very loud:

"I'm a dingle-dangle scarecrow
With a flippy-floppy hat.
I can shake my hands like this,
And I can shake my feet like that."

A king, on assuming his reign,
Exclaimed with a feeling of peign,
   "Though I'm legally heir,
   No one here seems to ceir
That I haven't been born with a breign."

A maid with a duster
Made a furious bluster
Dusting a bust in the hall.
When the bust it was dusted,
The bust it was busted,
The bust it was dust, that is all.

I saw Esau sawing wood, And Esau saw I saw him. Though Esau saw I saw him saw, Still Esau went on sawing.

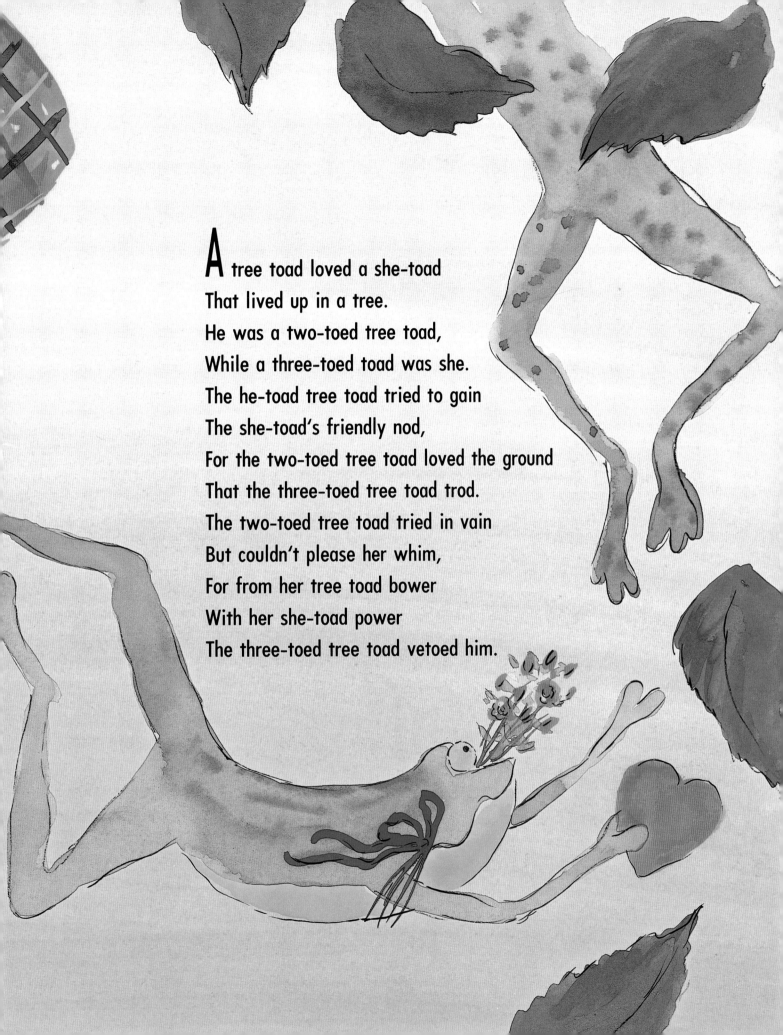

A tree toad loved a she-toad
That lived up in a tree.
He was a two-toed tree toad,
While a three-toed toad was she.
The he-toad tree toad tried to gain
The she-toad's friendly nod,
For the two-toed tree toad loved the ground
That the three-toed tree toad trod.
The two-toed tree toad tried in vain
But couldn't please her whim,
For from her tree toad bower
With her she-toad power
The three-toed tree toad vetoed him.

This little man lived all alone,
And he was a man of sorrow,
For if the weather was fair today,
He was sure it would rain tomorrow.

The fabulous wizard of Oz
Retired from business becoz
    What with up-to-date science,
    To most of his clients
He wasn't the wiz that he woz.

I know a house, and a cold old house,
A cold old house by the sea.
If I were a mouse in that cold old house,
What a cold, cold mouse I'd be!

There was a young lady of Ealing,
Who had a peculiar feeling
        That she was a fly
        And wanted to try
To walk upside down on the ceiling.

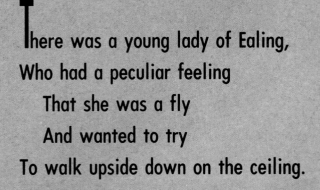

There are two things I can't get right,
No matter how I've tried:
I wind the cat up every night
And put the clock outside.

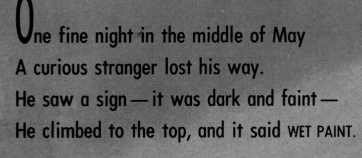

One fine night in the middle of May
A curious stranger lost his way.
He saw a sign — it was dark and faint —
He climbed to the top, and it said WET PAINT.

There was a young farmer of Leeds
Who swallowed six packets of seeds.
It soon came to pass
He was covered with grass,
And he couldn't sit down for the weeds.

There was an old woman called Nothing-at-all,
Who rejoiced in a dwelling exceedingly small:
A man stretched his mouth to its utmost extent,
And down at one gulp house and old woman went.

Way down yonder in the maple swamp
The wild geese gather and the ganders honk.
The mares kick up and the ponies prance,
The old sow whistles and the little pigs dance.

I love you, I love you, I love you, I do.
Don't get excited, I love monkeys, too!

If you see a monkey in a tree,
Don't throw sticks, it might be me.

John and a monkey
Sitting on a rail.
What is the difference?
John has no tail.

I've scratched the measles, itched the pox,
The mumps, they made me drool.
They weren't no fun, not any one—
But they got me out of school!

Row, row, row your boat
Gently down the stream,
Throw your teacher overboard
And listen to her scream.

Roses are red,
Violets are blue,
I copied your paper,
And I flunked too.

Ooey Gooey was a worm.
Ooey Gooey loved to squirm.
Squirmed up on the railroad track,
Squirmed around all on his back.
Along came a train, clickety-clack.
OOEY GOOEY!

Grandpa's whiskers long and gray,
Always getting in the way.
Grandma chews them in her sleep,
Thinking they are shredded wheat.

The elephant is a graceful bird,
It flits from twig to twig.
It builds its nest in a rhubarb tree
And whistles like a pig.

A hippo decided one day
That she would take up ballet,
  So she stood on her toes
  And said, "Okay, here goes!"
And fell back with a splash in the bay.

The witch flew out on Halloween,
Her hair was blue, her nose was green,
Her teeth the longest ever seen,
Oh, she was lovely, lovely, lovely!

Her cat was black and fit and fat,
He lashed his tail and humped his back,
He scritched and scratched and hissed and spat,
Oh, he was lovely, lovely, lovely!

They rode a cleaner, not a broom.
"Go left!" screeched Puss, and spoke their doom.
She turned right—they hit the moon.
Oh, it was lovely, lovely, lovely.

I am the old witch
Who lives by the wall,
And I have come to snatch you—
To snatch you, one and all.

I am the goblin
Who lives by the stall,
And I have come to fetch you—
To fetch you, one and all.

I am the ghostie
Who lives in the hall,
And I have come to catch you—
To catch you, one and all.

The night was growing cold
As she trudged through snow and sleet,
And her nose was long and cold,
And her shoes were full of feet.

The frost sprite always
Thinks it's fun
To play his pranks
On everyone.

He pinches ears
And cheeks and toes,
But where he's standing
No one knows.

He paints upon
The windowpane:
A flower, a bridge,
A vine, a chain.

He nips the leaves
Upon the trees,
This busy fellow
No one sees.

I know you little, I love you lots,
My love for you would fill ten pots,
Fifteen buckets, sixteen cans,
Three teacups, and four dishpans.

Ashes to ashes
Dust to dust
Oil those brains
Before they rust.

Down the street his funeral goes
As sobs and wails diminish.
He died from drinking straight shellac,
But he had a lovely finish.